The
White House

Tristan Boyer Binns

Heinemann Library
Chicago, Illinois

© 2001 Reed Educational & Professional Publishing
Published by Heinemann Library,
an imprint of Reed Educational & Professional Publishing,
Chicago, IL

Customer Service 888-454-2279

Visit our website at www.heinemannlibrary.com

Designed by Lisa Buckley
Printed in Hong Kong

05 04 03 02 01
10 9 8 7 6 5 4 3 2 1

Library of Congress Cataloging-in-Publication Data
Binns, Tristan Boyer, 1968-
     The White House / Tristan Boyer Binns.
          p. cm. -- (Symbols of freedom)
     Includes bibliographical references (p.) and index.
     ISBN 1-58810-122-3 (lib. bdg.)   ISBN 1-58810-406-0 (pbk. bdg.)
      1.White House (Washington, D.C.)--Juvenile literature. 2. Presidents--United
States--Juvenile literature. 3. Washington (D.C.)--Buildings, structures, etc.--Juvenile
literature. [1. White House (Washington, D.C.) 2. Presidents.] I. Title.

F204.W5 B56 2001
975.3--dc21
                                                                        00-058142

Acknowledgments
The author and publishers are grateful to the following for permission to reproduce copyright material: p.4 Charles O'Rear/Corbis, p.6 David Burnett/Contact Press Images/PictureQuest, p.7, 11 Richard T. Norwitz/Corbis, p.8 Robert Schaffer/Tony Stone Images, p.9, 15, 20, 22, 24, 25, 26, 27, 29 Bettemann/Corbis, p.10 Dennis Brack/Black Star Publishing/PictureQuest, p.12 National Geographic Society, p.13, 16 Wally McNamee, p.14, 17, 23 The White House Historical Society, p.18 The White House, p.19, 28 Library of Congress, p.21 Wood River Gallery/PictureQuest.
Cover photograph by Henryk Kaiser/eStock Photography/PictureQuest.

Every effort has been made to contact copyright holders of any material reproduced in this book. Any omissions will be rectified in subsequent printings if notice is given to the publisher.

Some words are shown in bold, **like this.**
You can find out what they mean by looking in the glossary.

Contents

The Most Famous House

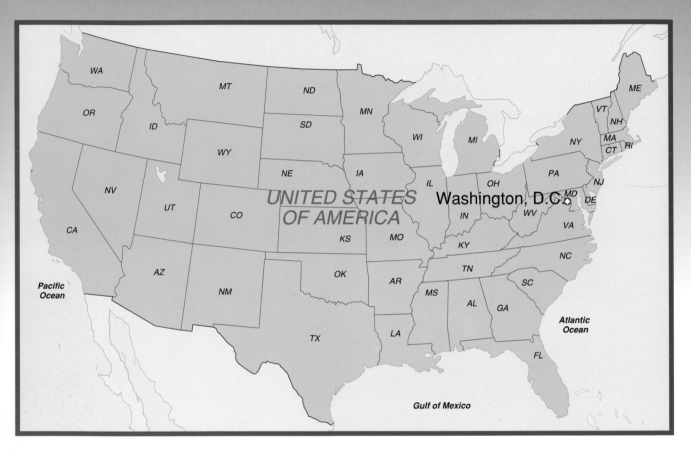

The White House is the best-known house in our country. It is in Washington, D.C., the **capital** of the United States.

The president of the United States lives in the White House. The president's family lives there, too. The president also works there with his **staff.**

A Busy House

Important people and leaders from other countries visit the White House. The president sometimes has big dinners to welcome them. **Ceremonies** are sometimes held there, too.

You can see the White House on television.
News reporters sometimes stand in front of it.
The president often makes speeches from the
White House.

Everyone's House

The president lives and works in the White House. But it really belongs to everyone in the country. Anyone can visit the White House. It does not cost any money to go in.

There is even a special party just for children.
Every year, children come to the White House
one Monday in spring. They roll Easter eggs
on the **lawn.**

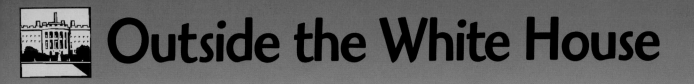

Outside the White House

The White House is bigger than most houses. It has two large porches called porticoes. The north portico is like a front porch. It is the one most often shown on television.

10

The White House also has **wings.** There is an East Wing and a West Wing. They are extra parts of the building. They hold offices for the president and his **staff.**

The White House is very big inside, too!
There are 132 rooms. There are public rooms
that everyone can go in.

Other rooms are just for the president and
his **staff.** There are rooms on the second floor
where the president and his family live.

Colorful Rooms

Some of the rooms are named after colors.
The Red Room has red walls and red **furniture**.
There is a Green and a Blue Room, too.

The biggest room in the White House is the East Room. It has fancy curtains and big **chandeliers.** It is used for big parties.

The Private Rooms

The Oval Office is a **private** room. The president does a lot of his work in this room. He also gives speeches for television there.

Some special visitors can stay in the private rooms. They can sleep in the Lincoln Bedroom. It has **furniture** that belonged to President Abraham Lincoln.

Animals in the White House

Many presidents and their families have had pets in the White House. President Bill Clinton had a dog named Buddy and a cat named Socks. Buddy and Socks even got mail!

President Benjamin Harrison's family had lots of pets. They had a pet goat named Old Whiskers. Old Whiskers once ran away with the president's grandchildren in a cart!

A House for the President

President George Washington never lived in the White House. But he was in charge of building the president's house. He wanted it to be a big, important house.

It took eight years to build the White House.
It was built of bricks and stone. The bricks
and stone were painted white.

Moving In

John Adams was the first president to live in the White House. When he moved in, the house was not done. Only six rooms inside were finished.

There was not much **furniture.** There were
no bathrooms or closets. The yard was
a mess. The East Room was used to dry the
president's laundry!

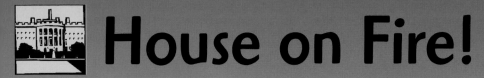# House on Fire!

Soon after the White House was built, the United States went to war. **British** soldiers set fire to the White House. The president and his wife had to run away.

The White House almost burned down.
Suddenly, it started to rain. The rain put out
the fire, but the house was ruined. It took
three years to build it again.

White House Changes

The White House has been standing for 200 years. There have been a lot of changes inside and out. But it is still a **symbol** of our strong country.

About 60 years ago, the White House was in very bad shape. Everything was taken out— even the walls and the floors! The whole inside of the house was built again.

The White House at War

Until the **Civil War,** the White House was the biggest house in America. During that war, soldiers lived in the East Room.

During **World War I,** there was no one to cut the grass at the White House. Sheep were put on the **lawn** to eat the grass!

Fact File

White House

The White House has
* 32 bathrooms
* 147 windows
* 412 doors
* 12 chimneys
* 3 elevators
* 1 swimming pool
* 1 movie theater
* 1 library
* 1 bowling alley
* 1 horseshoe pit
* 1 **putting green**

Until 1902,
the White House
was called the
Executive Mansion,
the President's House,
or the
President's Palace.

Glossary

British someone or something that comes from Britain

capital important city where the government is located

ceremony gathering of people for an important event

chandelier very large light that hangs from a ceiling

Civil War U.S. war in the 1800s, in which northern states fought against southern states

furniture tables, chairs, sofas, and other things people use in a room

lawn large area of grass that is planted and cared for outside a building or house

private not for everyone

putting green practice area for people who play golf

staff people who work in a place, such as an office

symbol something that stands for an idea

wing part of a building that is added on later to make the building bigger

World War I war that was fought from 1914 to 1918 in Europe

More Books to Read

An older reader can help you with these books:

Karr, Kathleen. *White House Trivia*. New York: Hyperion Books for Children, 1999.

Sandak, Cass R. *The White House*. Austin, Tex.: Raintree Steck-Vaughn, 2000.

Wilson, Jon. *The White House: 1600 Pennsylvania Avenue*. Chanhassen, Minn.: The Child's World, Inc., 1998.

Index